SUCCESSFULLY DESIGNING HYBRID PROJECT MANAGEMENT

WHY THE COMBINATION OF SCRUM WITH CONVENTIONAL PROJECT MANAGEMENT APPROACHES HARDLY ADDS ANY VALUE AND WHICH ALTERNATIVES HAVE BEEN PROVEN FOR YEARS.

JUSTUS M. DUMONT

Copyright © Justus M. Dumont
All Rights Reserved.

ISBN 978-1-63886-987-0

This book has been published with all efforts taken to make the material error-free after the consent of the author. However, the author and the publisher do not assume and hereby disclaim any liability to any party for any loss, damage, or disruption caused by errors or omissions, whether such errors or omissions result from negligence, accident, or any other cause.

While every effort has been made to avoid any mistake or omission, this publication is being sold on the condition and understanding that neither the author nor the publishers or printers would be liable in any manner to any person by reason of any mistake or omission in this publication or for any action taken or omitted to be taken or advice rendered or accepted on the basis of this work. For any defect in printing or binding the publishers will be liable only to replace the defective copy by another copy of this work then available.

Contents

Foreword	v
1. Taylorism	1
2. Surviving In The Vuca World	4
3. The Hybrid Challenge	12
4. Dsdm ® - Agile Project Management: An Introduction To The Framework	14
5. Dsdm As A Hybrid Alternative	35
6. Afterword	38
Bibliography	39

Foreword

Since I've been managing projects - and have been doing so for well over twenty years - I've always run up against certain limits. Far too many projects go wrong. There are statistics which state that in Europe around 80% of all projects are not completed within the parameters agreed at the start of the project, and far too many projects are either not completed at all or do not achieve the target on which they are based. If you consider this figure to be even somewhat realistic, you have to ask yourself whether project management makes any sense at all. Who would entrust someone with a task in everyday life if they had to reckon with the probability of partial or complete failure being so considerable?

Now, one could simply assume that project managers or the methods and frameworks they use might not be all that good. While it can be assumed that not all project managers are equally well trained and equally experienced, such a large number of "failures" is statistically rather unlikely. So it makes sense to look for other reasons.

From my experience, many reasons exist for project failure. However, one thing must always be kept in mind: Projects are not implemented in a focused manner and in many cases are worked on by people alongside their day-to-day business. In many organizations, anyone who can control some money can launch a project uncoordinated, without ensuring that the project makes sense in the overall context of the organization and its goals. Resources are assigned from the normal teams and are expected to do the project work on the side. In the process, responsibility is readily shifted to a project manager.

FOREWORD

In some organizations, there is a real ostrich policy here. Several colleagues who are "bought in" as external project managers for such projects tell me about a wide variety of projects for which they are supposed to send regular status reports to their steering committee or a program office. However, it is clear to everyone in the company: If you report "green", everything is fine; if you report "yellow" or even "red" - even if you provide a clear strategy for remedying the grievance - then you have to find a new client. Result: Report "green" until even the dumbest person can no longer ignore the problem, and look for a new project in parallel. The result is clear: projects that cannot be completed or can only be completed with considerable additional effort.

In short: Project management offers a great challenge for the client and its organization, the project control and the people who realize the deliverables. Leadership problems in organizations manifest themselves here very much, but also the disadvantages of teams which do not identify with the project and its goals because they are not "taken along for the ride".

This book will not focus on these topics. However, I do not want to simply gloss over them because I see how fundamentally important they are for the success of projects.

Rather, I would like to address a structural challenge of projects. Many organizations increasingly rely on agile frameworks and methods. Scrum, in particular, is experiencing a steady increase in the number of organizations using this framework. However, there are many misunderstandings because many mistakenly think Scrum is an agile project management framework. This is especially impressive because there is a central statement of Scrum, which is, "There is no project manager."

Those who "bring Scrum in-house" can achieve tremendous benefits in terms of productivity, quality, agility and employee motivation if they introduce it correctly and do not see Scrum merely as a toolbox, but understand that it is based on a certain idea of values and mindset. Only when these ideas - beyond the Scrum team - are lived, Scrum can unfold its full benefits.

However, Scrum is in no way a method or a framework for project control and project controlling etc. When users realize this, they try to compensate for these (supposed) disadvantages by combining Scrum with existing project management methods. In most cases, this is not so much a "win-win" as a "lose-lose" combination, because both participants have to give up or adapt central tasks and success factors.

This is exactly where this book comes in. Let's find out together whether this has to be the case or whether there is an alternative that realizes a true "win-win" relationship and thus combines the best of project management and agile development, so to speak.

I welcome you on the journey together

The author

I
Taylorism

The term "Taylorism" is often used very negatively today, especially in the context of agile companies. Frederick Winslow Taylor himself would most likely speak of process control ("task management") in connection with his research. He rejected the terms "scientific management" and "Taylor management" that are often used today in connection with his name.

In fact, the term process control can also give us a clearer picture of what Taylor was really about and the context in which his findings should be seen.

His findings are often attributed to the following[1]:

1. *The external (e.g. suppliers) and internal (e.g. workflows) processes of a company can be calculated and controlled.*
2. *The work can be separated into executive and planning work.*
3. *Workers and machines merely perform individual functions (specialization) that can be centrally planned and controlled (centralization).*

4. *Using scientific methods, it is possible to determine the best way to perform a work step.*
5. *The necessary operations to manufacture a product consist of a specific and definable sequence of execution functions.*
6. *People work simply to earn money.*

Whether we like or dislike the approaches communicated by these points, they correspond to the spirit of the times and the economic and social realities of the period in which they were formulated. We are in an environment where we speak of a push approach to product creation. Machines were expensive and only economically viable if they could be used to the maximum. Every standstill meant production losses on the one hand, but of course also that the amortization of the corresponding investments failed to materialize. In this context, it was correspondingly important to have a production approach that ensured that production virtually never came to a standstill. To make this possible, certain issues were of fundamental importance:

ax. Clearly defined processes mean that tasks can be performed by anyone.
ax. Mastery of tools is an important prerequisite for this.
ax. To ensure that steps and procedures are traceable, comprehensive documentation is a basic requirement.
ax. This requires clear arrangements and agreements (contracts) between the organizations and individuals involved.
ax. This requires clear, reliable plans.

These are exactly the points that are on the right side of the word "more than" in the agile manifesto:

*"Individuals and interactions **more than** processes and tools*

*Functioning software **more than** comprehensive documentation*

*Cooperation with the customer **more than** contract negotiation*

*Responding to change **more than** following a plan [2]"*

Many organizations still essentially function according to these approaches today, and if we look closely, we see that many framework conditions such as laws and government structures also correspond to this mindset and approach. It has made various national economies successful and large over decades and has led to many organizations gaining an international reputation and global markets. However, today we find that many of these large corporations in industry, finance, etc. are increasingly facing new challenges and quite a few have long since been outflanked and taken over by foreign entrants, some of which are only a few years old. Many companies are facing the challenges of a VUCA world.

---

[1]Source: https://de.wikipedia.org/wiki/Scientific_Management (accessed 1/2021)

[2]Source: http://agilemanifesto.org/iso/de/manifesto.html (accessed 1/2021)

II

Surviving in the VUCA world

Although the term "VUCA world" originated at the United States Army War College (USAWC) in the 1990s, it is not a military term, but rather a description of what has increasingly manifested itself in the world in recent decades. VUCA stands for volatility (volatility), uncertainty (uncertainty), complexity (complexity) and ambiguity (ambiguity).

What is meant by this now? The world has become "smaller" in recent decades. We speak of globalization and mean by this that markets, but also social phenomena, no longer affect only the region, the country or, at best, the continent, but that we find ourselves in an environment where changes on another continent can affect local markets and customer needs. Technical constraints, which were partly due to scientific progress and partly due to capital intensity - in terms of acquiring modern infrastructure - are increasingly falling away. Small businesses on another continent can suddenly compete successfully against billion-dollar corporations by using computing and production resources from the Internet, and often respond more quickly and efficiently. Requirements have reached a level of complexity that can no longer be handled in the form of linear processes. The multitude of mutual influencing variables means that simple cause-and-effect relationships are often no longer able to explain interrelationships and make them controllable.

In such an environment, the approaches of Taylorism no longer lead to the desired results. More and more companies have discovered this, sometimes painfully. It has long been the case that it is no longer the "big guy" who eats the "little guy", but the "fast guy" who eats the "slow guy". In such a context, large structures and long decision-making paths are absolutely counterproductive, and clearly defined, documented processes often no longer provide a competitive advantage because the number of options and changes is far too extensive.

The world has changed and only gradually are we succeeding in adapting the associated framework in terms of legal regulations, training, procedures, etc. to this "VUCA world".

Cynefin framework

The Cynefin framework was developed in 1999 in the context of knowledge management and organizational strategy by Mary E. Boone and Dave Snowden. It is a knowledge management model with the task of describing problems, situations and systems. Four domains and an additional one are used. The four domains are called:

- **Clear**, in which the relationship between cause and effect is obvious to all.
- **Complicated**, in which the relationship between cause and effect requires analysis, another form of testing, and/or the application of expertise.
- **Complex**, in which the relationship between cause and effect can only be perceived in retrospect, but not in advance.
- **Chaotic**, in which there is no relationship between cause and effect at the system level (but there is in the system environment, but it cannot be experienced).

The fifth domain is titled "**Disorder**". It characterizes the domain of not knowing the nature of the applicable causality.

In our context, Clear and Chaotic are less relevant. Clear, obvious processes of cause and effect do not normally require much effort in terms of project control, while chaotic situations cannot be addressed with standardized procedures. Accordingly, in the context of project control, the domains "Complicated" and "Complex" are particularly relevant.

Complicated stands for a situation which may be characterized by many influencing factors, but whose cause-and-effect structure can still be clearly recognized. It can also be planned accordingly. The approach adapted according to the framework is "Sense - Analyze - Respond" - i.e. the perception and analysis of the situation and the formulation of procedures based on this. This corresponds to an approach of classical project management. We are here in the framework of the approaches of Tayloristic systems.

In a complex environment, however, the situation is completely different. Where cause-effect relationships can only be perceived in retrospect, appropriate planning based on defined processes and procedures is not expedient. Instead, it is necessary to react adequately to the situation. This is also illustrated in the approach of the Cynefin framework. It is characterized as "Probe - Sense - Respond". We are in a VUCA context. The experience and knowledge of stakeholders is critical. Stakeholders must find the framework conditions to be able to react quickly and purposefully based on external circumstances. However, this requires an organization that offers the appropriate framework conditions.

Theory X and Theory Y

In 1960, MIT professor Douglas MacGregor coined the term Theory X. It assumes that humans are lazy by nature and will do anything to avoid work. Man is extrinsically motivated and accordingly can only be guided by rewards and sanctions.

In addition, MacGregor also formulated a Theory Y. This propagates a completely different view of human beings. It says: People are ambitious and willing to work hard to achieve meaningful goals and also to apply self-discipline and self-control. They see work as a source of satisfaction and feel motivated by their performance and the successes achieved as a result. These people live a sense of responsibility and creativity.

However, MacGregor was not so much talking about what people are like in themselves, but rather about two different images of people as they are lived out by many superiors and organizations in relation to their employees.

His observation: Regardless of which image of man was represented, the superiors were always right. Their assessment was more or less a self-fulfilling prophecy. Whatever the superiors' view of their own employees was, they were right. Those who saw their employees as work-shy lazybones without motivation and initiative were just as right as those who saw them as hard-working and self-motivated, proactive people.

The explanation is not rooted in the person of the employee, but in that of the supervisor, who will lead his employees based on his own image of man. If he himself believes in employees of theory A, he will also lead them in this way: clear instructions, close monitoring, positive reinforcement in the case of success and clear sanctions in the case of mistakes. This will lead to the fact that his coworkers will adhere exactly to the existing instructions. They know that any deviation carries the risk of sanctions. Their self-perception is that of the executors of their supervisor's instructions in his project. Identification with the project and its goals is not to be expected, and own initiatives or even suggestions are only to be expected if they are demanded by special programs. A team feeling hardly arises, since everyone works to fulfill even the own defaults of the boss. Synergies are not asked for and are not measured, so they are of no use. The superior thus experiences exactly the cooperation that he always suspected, and thus feels strengthened in his assessment and will accordingly lead in this way in the future.

The supervisor with the Theory Y view of human nature will not be disappointed either. Since he places great trust in the initiative and commitment, but also the abilities of his employees, he will lead in a completely different way. He is deeply convinced of his employees' abilities and willingness to perform and will do everything in his power to enable them to achieve the agreed goals. His role is that of a coach who supports his team in their work and ensures that the employees have the framework conditions they need to achieve their goals. If necessary, he is available with advice and information. His team will appreciate the freedom and opportunity to participate and perceive the joint project as HIS project. Employees perceive that they are successful by working together as a team and that they have better ideas together as a result of the exchange. They gladly accept the coaching and support of their superiors through feedback and know-how. Their supervisor experiences a team of people as Theory Y describes them. Accordingly, he feels reinforced in his assessment and will continue and further develop his leadership style.

If we place these two theories in the context of Cynefin domains, the supervisor and team from Theory X better fit the domain 'Complicated', while those from the context of Theory Y better fit a team facing a VUCA challenge.

Outcome and output

Finally, we should also deal with the project focus. Often, no distinction is made here and it is actually assumed that classic project management and agile approach/framework are just two different "methods". This may be the case in individual cases. However, from a fundamental point of view, it is clear that both approaches serve completely different levels.

In classic project management, the focus is on developing products - these can be physical or virtual products. Agile development, on the other hand, tends to be about achieving benefits for the customer. This can -

and usually does - come about through the development of a specific product. In fact, however, a completely different product may develop during implementation than what was originally envisioned.

The reason is simple: In classical project management, the project is generally used to realize a previously defined specification. The actual, creative process of defining what is to be realized usually precedes the project. Agile projects, on the other hand, are based on the idea of realizing a vision. One could also say that it is about achieving a defined benefit. How this benefit is realized can change during the course of the project. This happens on the basis of an ongoing evaluation of the solution already implemented and feedback from the stakeholders involved. Thus, the creative process of defining the end product becomes part of the development process itself.

Planning and monitoring

Classic project management is often referred to as waterfall project management. Although different frameworks and approaches are subsumed under this (V-model, spiral model, etc.), the approaches essentially have a common basic structure, which consists of first defining the requirements to be implemented and then implementing them in the course of several phases. We thus assume a linear process flow.

If we use agile project management instead, we find that we are working to realize a vision. This vision denotes a state In the future. Be it that an existing problem has been solved or that, for example, a product has been implemented or finally a situation in which a new product or a new benefit for customers has been realized. The type of solution does not have to be fixed yet, rather there is the possibility that this will only develop in the course of the implementation.

Whereas classical project management focuses on the implementation of an already defined product, in the context of agile product development this product is only created in the course of the development process itself. In classical terms, one could say that classical project management is concerned with the realization of output, while agile development focuses on the realization of outcome (benefit).

This in turn means that completely different methods of project monitoring are appropriate. In the context of classic project management, the primary concern is to track whether the existing plan was adhered to and where any deviations occurred. In the context of agile project management, on the other hand, the created product itself is considered and the insights gained in the course of feedback become the basis for new requirements or for changing existing ones.

III
The hybrid challenge

In the corporate context, we often encounter very different objectives. On the one hand, there are requirements, for example, from the compliance context, which emphasize traceability, controlling, clear planning structures, etc., and on the other hand, there are requirements from the business context. are important. On the other hand, we want to be able to work with maximum agility in order to respond to changing conditions. Thus, there is a classic conflict of objectives. While on the one hand we demand a clearly defined service catalog, on the other hand the solution should be able to flexibly respond to and reflect changing requirements due to newly gained knowledge. The combination of both requirements is inherently contradictory and accordingly not feasible.

Nevertheless, many companies demand exactly that. This is often understood under the term "hybrid project management". It involves a combination of classic project management while retaining all the associated advantages in terms of plannability, security and traceability, and agile product development and the associated advantages in terms of agility and flexibility.

Of course, the requirements for hybrid project management are manifold. Different organizations, industries and company sizes have different needs that they associate with the keyword "hybrid project management". Nevertheless, there are some requirements that most companies express. Important aspects are:

- Clearly defined roles and responsibilities
- Clear project planning (in terms of money, time)
- Clearly defined delivery items
- Targeted reporting
- Adapted risk and quality management
- Flexible adaptation to changing requirements
- High degree of identification of the employees involved
- Maximum customer benefit
- Favorable and fast project implementation

These are just some of the most frequently expressed requirements for hybrid project management. In the following part, we want to examine a specific method that has proven itself in projects to see to what extent it meets these requirements. This is the DSDM method (Dynamic System Development Method), which is already one of the most frequently used project management methods in some European countries and which many users claim to be the most hybrid project management method.

IV

DSDM ® - Agile Project Management: An Introduction to the Framework

The basics

DSDM ®[1]stands for Dynamics Systems Development Method and is a further development of RAD (Rapid Application Development), based on the experience that this agile approach was very successful in terms of implementation speed and integration of employees from different areas into powerful teams, but lacked actual project control.

The first approaches of DSDM can be found in the first half of the nineties of the last century and have been continuously developed since then. Thus, DSDM Atern was initially created as the first version of the project framework; this has since been replaced in a further generation by AgilePF, which provides the basis for the training courses available today: AgilePM (Agile Project Manager), AgileBA (Agile Business Analyst), AgileDS (Agile Digital Services) and AgilePgM (Agile Program Management). These terms represent the different role trainings and application areas. This framework is becoming increasingly widespread, and there are reports that the number of people getting certified in the context of DSDM is already said to exceed the number of new Prince2 ® certifications in some European countries. However, since many certifiers are very cautious with these numbers, I could not verify this statement so far.

DSDM is based on a simple philosophy. It is:

"The greatest business value occurs when projects are aligned with clear business goals, deliver regular results, and involve the collaboration of motivated and empowered people."

DSDM attaches great importance to projects being carried out with DSDM based on common sense and pragmatic decisions. Accordingly, DSDM does not try to describe all possible use cases and options individually (which is not successful in practice anyway), but formulates eight principles which provide a good basis for decisions in the course of the project in order to really use DSDM in a target-oriented way within the framework of a continuous improvement process.

The eight principles are called:

1. Focus on the business need
2. Deliver on time
3. Work together
4. Do not tolerate any compromise in terms of quality
5. Build step by step on solid foundations
6. Develop iteratively
7. Communicate continuously and clearly
8. Demonstrate control

As a complete project management method, DSDM has the framework practiced by most methods of processes and their tasks, roles and responsibilities, and products to control the process. Products may sound somewhat foreign to some in this context. However, the choice of words is accurate. These are elements such as reports, registers, displays or similar, which are created in the course of the project by people involved in the project. These elements are not primarily made for delivery to the customer - as what we would commonly understand as a product - but are needed for the control and execution of the project itself.

We will look at the above elements in more detail below:

The process

The project management process of DSDM is not much different from the one known from Prince2, for example. It is also a development process managed in process phases with the phases:

- Pre-Project
- Feasibility phase (feasibility phase)
- Foundations phase (basic phase)

- Evolutionary Design (development phase)
- Deployment phase (delivery phase)
- Post-Project (after the project)

In the pre-project phase, it should be ensured that only those projects are started which can also achieve the intended goal. Based on the results of the work, a decision is made as to whether the project is to be pursued further or whether it is to be terminated at this stage, thus saving the expense of further work.

In the subsequent feasibility phase, it is determined whether the project is technically feasible and economically viable from a business perspective. If this is not the case, the project can still be stopped before further expenses are incurred.

In the Foundations phase, on the one hand, a solid understanding of the purpose of the project is to be ensured by all parties involved. In addition, the products and plans for implementation are created. The planning is only so detailed that it does not hinder the agile implementation in the course of the implementation phases. In smaller projects, the Feasibility and Foundations phases can coincide, and in more complex projects, it is possible to enter the next implementation cycle with a new Foundations phase after the Deployment phases.

After the foundation has been laid in this way, implementation takes place in the form of development cycles, which are called timeboxes in DSDM. It can be assumed that decision-making powers are distributed within the project based on the prioritization of requirements. More detailed information on this will be presented in the section on MoSCow prioritization.

As usual in the context of agile decision-making, development is characterized by short development cycles, feedback rounds and continuous learning. An increment is developed, which is then delivered as part of the deployment phase. The project is then formally completed with the last release.

During the post-project phase, which takes place after the project life cycle, the extent to which the project is able to realize the goals planned for it is examined.

MoSCoW - the hybrid decision

MoSCow prioritization is used in various contexts. Here MoSCoW stands for

- MUST - represent the MUST, the Minimum Usable SubseT, i.e. those requirements that are guaranteed to be implemented because their omission would call into question the justification of the project.
- SHOULD - Requirements which are implemented under normal circumstances and provide significant benefit to the organization.
- COULD - requirements, which are implemented whenever possible; however, since they are the least important of the three categories to the client, they are the first to be neglected when problems arise.
- WON'T - Requirements that may be important in the future but are not currently considered.

MoSCoW prioritization is an essential aspect of the DSDM planning process. Where it can be assumed that in the context of Could requirements there may well be significant changes up to and including elimination or even new requirements, those at MUST level are relatively stable. Decision-making authority is also distributed accordingly based on prioritization, where the solution development team can essentially respond to changes in the context of could requirements itself within the scope of product development, whereas planning and decisions for higher-priority requirements remain at the project management level. This also takes into account the fact that requirements in the detailed area and with less central requirements are subject to much greater change and at the same time have much less influence on the overall benefit of the project than those at MUST level. Thus, such decisions also have no fundamental influence on the project and, on the other hand, can be made and approached in a very pragmatic and goal-oriented manner.

Accordingly, responsibilities and decision-making powers are also assigned appropriately within the framework of the role model.

The roles

The organizational structure of DSDM is based on two levels: the project level and the solution delivery team level. The roles at the project level are responsible for managing the project, whereas the roles at the level of the Solution Development Team are dedicated to day-to-day business and, within the scope of the agreed authority, also make decisions independently with regard to adjustments and changes - as long as these do not result in adjustments that go beyond their scope of decision-making.

The special feature of the DSDM role model is that the Solution Development Team does not consist exclusively of technically oriented roles whose task is essentially to implement decisions made by the roles at project level. Rather, the solution development team comprises roles of all orientations from "business" to "technology" to roles with a management and process focus. To enable projects of different sizes to be implemented with DSDM, a role can be taken on by several people or one person can occupy several roles.

This lays a solid foundation for ensuring that decisions can always be made at the appropriate level, both at the project level and in the context of the individual development cycles, which means that the solution development team can react quickly to changes in day-to-day business and make its own decisions in the process. At the same time, it is still ensured that overall control at the project level is not impaired by this and that both the agreed goals can be implemented and the framework conditions can be met. In short, we have a solid project management system that is ideally combined with an agile approach and thus "combines the best of both worlds".

Now let's take a closer look at the role model:

The basis of a successful project lies in the cooperation of the people involved in it. DSDM assigns clear roles and responsibilities to the people involved in a project. In this context, good cooperation between the various roles is crucial.

The best solutions come from self-organizing, empowered teams that know and accept their responsibilities.

DSDM distinguishes 4 different areas of interest:

- Roles focused on business interests, i.e. roles that represent the views and needs of the company

- Representatives of the solution-specific and technical interests
- Roles focused on management interests, i.e., roles that reflect the views of management and company representation
- Roles with focus on process interests, i.e. roles that focus on the process

In addition, DSDM distinguishes roles on different levels:

- Project-level roles collectively have the authority to lead the project.

They may be part of a project board or steering committee and are often composed of directors, managers, or coordinators of the project work. They are responsible for steering the project or working with steering authorities outside the project. All project-level roles must adopt a supportive, empowering leadership style.

- Roles of the solution development team together form the "engine room" of the project.

They implement the solution and also ensure the appropriate quality control. Within a project, there can also be several solution development teams working in parallel, with all roles represented in each of them so that the associated responsibilities are also covered.

1. Supporting roles provide support as needed throughout the project lifecycle. Roles can be taken by one or more people as needed.

A role is not necessarily synonymous with a person. A person can take on several roles depending on the circumstances of the project. Likewise, it is possible for a role to be taken on by several people in parallel. If a role is covered by several people, close communication between the people concerned is crucial.

The roles at project level

The business sponsor

The Business Sponsor represents the top business function at the project level. He is the main project owner and responsible for the project, the proposed solution and the applied implementation approach. He is responsible for the business case and the project budget. In order to make business issues and financial decisions, he must hold a high enough position within the organization.

The Business Visionary

The Business Visionary has a senior business role at the project level. The role should always be held by a single person who has a clear vision for the project. The business visionary is more actively involved in the project than the business sponsor and represents the sponsor's needs and views in day-to-day business. He also ensures that this vision is appropriately reflected in the business case. He remains involved throughout the project, providing strategic direction to the team and ensuring that the solution is implemented according to the business case.

Technical Coordinator

The Technical Coordinator ensures a consistent way of working for the solution specific and technical roles. He or she ensures that goal-oriented technical decisions are made based on current technology. The Technical Coordinator fulfills the same function from a technical perspective as the Business Visionary from a business perspective.

The Project Manager

The project manager coordinates the project and leads the solution development team at a rough level. This means that we are not dealing with a manager who gets involved in micromanagement. This role is about the big picture and achieving the agreed upon goals. The project manager is aware that he or she must leave the planning and implementation at the detailed level to the solution development team to enable optimal results. This requires an agile, supportive management style rather than a "command and control" style.

The Project Manager carries out his responsibilities throughout the project. It includes both the economic and technical aspects of project implementation in all project phases.

The roles at solution development team level

The Business Analyst

The Business Analyst supports the roles at the project level, but is also fully integrated into the Solution Development team. He supports the collaboration of business and technical roles and facilitates the realization of appropriate decisions on the evolving solution.

The active involvement of the later users of the solution is crucial for solution development. The business analyst provides support to facilitate communication between the roles involved.

The Business Ambassador

The Business Ambassador is the most important representative of the company within the Solution Development Team. In the Foundations phase, he makes a significant contribution to formulating and prioritizing requirements.

After the requirements have been agreed upon and a first version has been created (by the end of the Foundations phase), the Business Ambassador presents the daily details of the requirements within the timeboxes. He can draw on his own experience or that of the business advisor.

In Evolutionary Design, the Business Ambassador makes the decisions necessary in the day-to-day business on behalf of the company.

For this reason, it is important that the business ambassador has the necessary knowledge and skills as well as the acceptance and authority to make such decisions, which are subsequently supported by all parties involved.

The team leader

The Team Leader is the servant-leader of the Solution Development Team. This means that he or she does not lead the team as a subordinate, but sees his or her responsibility in ensuring that the team can work optimally. This involves supporting the relevant processes, but also creating the framework conditions and accompanying the team in its daily work.

The Team Leader works with the team to plan and coordinate all aspects of product implementation at the detailed level. The Team Leader is ideally elected by his or her colleagues in the Solution Development Team.

The person who can optimally lead the team in a particular phase of the project is chosen. Accordingly, it is common for the team leader to take on one or more other roles in the solution development team in addition to this role.

The Solution Developers

The solution developers, together with the other roles of the solution development team, jointly implement the solution increment.

This should meet the functional and non-functional needs of the business.

The Solution Testers

Solution testers are an integral part of the solution development team.

You will perform testing during the project in accordance with the agreed testing strategy.

The supporting roles

The Business Advisor

In organizational terms, the Business Advisor is often a colleague of the Business Ambassador.

As a business subject matter expert, provides specific and often expert input into solution development or testing.

The business advisor is often a future user or beneficiary of the solution. In some cases, he or she also communicates legal or regulatory requirements for the solution.

The Technical Advisor

The Technical Advisor supports the team by providing technical input to the project.

The role is often filled by people from the area of operational implementation of the changes, support or from the area of maintenance of the future solution.

The workshop facilitator

The Workshop Facilitator is responsible for planning, organizing and conducting workshops.

It ensures that the objectives set in advance are achieved within the framework planned for the workshops. It should be independent of the results achieved.

The DSDM Coach

The DSDM coach supports the team in understanding DSDM and performing their tasks according to the DSDM approach.

The products

DSDM has a set of 14 products that can be used in the course of a project. Products can be reports, running protocols or even plans. Of course, the developing project is also a product. However, this is a proposal, which can also be reduced in the context of the adaptation to the project or can be different in the implementation with regard to the degree of formality. It is conceivable, for example, that a report with low formality can be made in the form of a telephone call or an e-mail, if this is so agreed.

Here, too, we find the pragmatic view of the procedure already mentioned at the beginning. The product model describes the responsibility for the individual products, the time of their creation and further development, and the goals pursued with them.

DSDM differentiates products according to the context in which they are used into business-oriented, process-oriented (management-oriented) and solution-oriented (product-oriented) products.

Business oriented products

Terms of Reference

The Terms of Reference provide a rough definition of the business focus and ultimate goals of the project. The primary objective is to provide a clear delineation of scope for the Feasibility Phase. The Terms of Reference are considered a steering product (letter "G") because they can be used to help prioritize the project within a portfolio.

Business Case

The business case provides the basis or justification for the project from a business perspective. The business vision describes a changed company and how it is expected to develop incrementally until the project is completed.

The justification is usually based on an investment calculation, which compares the expected benefits with the expected costs for production and operation (total cost of ownership).

The business case is created as a rough draft at the end of the feasibility phase and then further developed until the end of the foundation phase. There it represents an element for approval of the development. At the end of each project increment, it is formally checked whether the business case is still realistic.

Prioritised Requirements List (PRL)

The PRL roughly describes the requirements that the project must fulfill. It shows their priority in terms of meeting the project goals and business needs.

The consideration of requirements begins in the Feasibility Phase and a version of the PRL defines the project scope at the end of the Foundations Phase.

Subsequently, new requirements and findings will result in adjustments that must be formally managed to ensure alignment with the project's corporate vision and scope is maintained.

Benefits Assessment

The benefits assessment takes place after the end of the project. This evaluates the benefits that have actually resulted from the project outcome.

If the benefits according to the business case occur over a longer period of time, it may make sense to conduct several benefits assessments at regular intervals.

Solution oriented products

Solutions Architecture Definition

It provides a rough design framework for the solution.

In doing so, it covers both economic and technical aspects of the solution in a level of detail that leaves sufficient scope for design in the course of development.

Development Approach Definition

It provides a rough definition of the tools, techniques, methods and standards that will be applied during the development.

A central aspect here is how the quality of the solution can be guaranteed. For this reason, the strategy of testing measures represents a central component of the development approach, which is described in the Development Approach Definition.

The Evolving Solution

The Evolving Solution consists of all components of the final solution as well as the intermediate solutions that are necessary to develop the solution. The components contained in it change their status in the course of development.

This also includes models, prototypes, supporting materials, and test artifacts. At the end of each project increment, the solution increment is transferred to operational use and thus becomes the deployed solution.

Management oriented products

Delivery Plan
The Delivery Plan represents the rough schedule for the individual increments of a project and also records, at least initially, the timeboxes that make it up.

The Delivery Plan does not represent a detailed plan, as this is created by the Solution- Development team members in Evolutionary-Development.

Management Approach Definition
The management approach definition captures the management approach for the project.

It records how the project is planned and organized, how stakeholders are involved, and how progress is demonstrated.

The management definition is outlined during the Feasibility phase and further refined during the Foundation phase. As changes occur during the project, the outline is updated.

Feasibility Assessment
At the end of the project phase of the same name, the Feasibility Assessment provides an overview of the business, solution and management products developed within it.

Each product should be sufficiently mature to allow a decision to be made as to whether or not the project has a high probability of feasibility. The document can be designed either as a versioned collection of the included products or as a summary of the important aspects included in it.

Foundations Summary

Like the Feasibility Assessment at the end of the Feasibility Phase, the Foundation Summary at the end of the Foundations Phase provides an interim status of the development of the business, solution and management products.

The individual products should be sufficiently elaborated to allow a meaningful decision to be made as to whether the project has a high probability of delivering the expected benefits. It can also be designed either as a collection of the included products or as a summary.

Timebox plan

The Timebox Plan presents the details of a single timebox as identified in the Delivery Plan. It documents the objectives and detailed deliverables for that timebox, along with the activities to produce the deliverables and the resources required to achieve them.

The timebox schedule is set up by the Solution Development team and frequently displayed on a team board in the form of pending, ongoing and completed tasks. The timebox schedule is updated at least once a day as part of the Daily Standup.

Timebox Review Records

The timebox review records feedback from the review at the end of a timebox. It describes what has been achieved and represents feedback that could impact future development.

Where appropriate, auditable comments from competent business advisors and other roles make this document the steering product.

Project Review Report

The Project Review Report is a document that is completed at the end of each product increment by adding new sections related to that increment.

It includes the following main topics:

- The feedback from the testing of the implemented solution
- The learning from the retrospective to the respective increment
- If applicable, already realized business benefits from the implemented solution

After the last product increment, a retrospective on the entire project is conducted as part of a project closing, which is also partly based on the records of the individual product increments.

DSDM in practice

Let's now take a closer look at the individual points from our "specifications" for a hybrid project management solution:

- Clearly defined roles and responsibilities

DSDM has a very distinctive role model with responsibilities at both project and implementation level. Thereby, it is possible to adapt the existing model to projects of different sizes and objectives within the scope of the adaptation to the project by splitting and combining roles.

- Clear project planning (money, time)

DSDM has a classic project phase model, which can be adapted to different project sizes during implementation. Independently of this, planning takes place on two levels, which make it possible to practice a clear project structure and reliable control on the one hand, and to respond quickly and flexibly to changing framework conditions in day-to-day business on the other.

- Clearly defined delivery items

If we relate this to the product (or multiple products) that are to be delivered by the project, a unique combination of possibilities is found with the DSDM approach. On the one hand, what is to be delivered is clearly defined at a high level, and on the other hand, there is a high degree of flexibility and customization possibilities at the detailed level in order to be able to optimally respond to changing framework conditions and situations within the implementation order. In this way, we have combined the "best of both worlds", so to speak.

- Targeted reporting

In DSDM, reports, plans and reports are also described under the term "products". The self-expandable (or customizable) set of fourteen such products provides the foundation for the kind of sophisticated reporting often required in the context of large organizations and products, but can also be readily adapted for smaller projects in less formal contexts. In addition, it is also possible to supplement the existing set of products with further, organization-specific ones. However, the question of the usefulness of reports and documents should always be kept in mind, as this always leads to effort in the creation and administration, which only makes sense if it is also countered by a concrete benefit that justifies the effort.

- Adapted risk and quality management

Like many project management methods, DSDM does not have its own risk or quality management approach or corresponding processes. However, both aspects are sufficiently covered within the processes and, where this is not sufficient, can be supplemented by processes of the corresponding approaches lived in the organization or project environment. An additional aspect in the context of project risk assessment is covered by the PAQ - the Project Assessment Questionnaire - which is used in the context of DSDM projects in several target-oriented ways.

- Flexible adaptation to changing requirements

Adaptation to changing requirements is represented within the framework of the division of decision-making authority based on the various levels of action. In addition, the readiness to adapt even far-reaching requirements is part of the method and defined by suitable processes. An important component of this is the possibility, already provided for, of recourse to a further Foundations phase for the implementation of an adaptation to requirements identified during deployment.

- High degree of identification of the employees involved

Of course, a particular method - whether agile or not - does not provide a sufficient basis for employee identification. However, a framework that practices co-determination and the joint development of solutions in a team, as well as values and principles based on this, undoubtedly offers good support in ensuring that people involved in the project see it as "their" project, which is an essential prerequisite for identification.

- Maximum customer benefit

Customer benefit is actually always very much at the center of the approach in agile approaches. This is also the case with DSDM. On the one hand, this is expressed in the fact that a system is built in order to react optimally to adaptations of requirements on the part of the customer, but on the other hand also in a profound inclusion of the customer and his needs in the structure of the decision-making and implementation processes and the associated role and responsibility model.

- Favorable and fast project implementation

DSDM offers a concept for the implementation of projects within fixed time and cost frames without sacrificing quality. Measures such as a focus on the earliest possible delivery of beneficial interim results additionally enable the possibility of an early realization of benefits and, if applicable, also of revenues.

---

[1]For the sake of easier readability, the ® designation is omitted in the following in relation to DSDM, to the DSDM products (AgilePM ® etc.) as well as in relation to other methods such as Prince2 ® after a single mention in the following text, but is always considered to be included.

V
DSDM as a hybrid alternative

Having looked a little closer at DSDM, let's conclude by looking at how it relates to Scrum, the most widely used agile framework, and how it relates to traditional project management:

DSDM ® or Scrum?

Again and again I encounter the misunderstanding that DSDM is quasi an alternative to Scrum. This is not the case, as the Scrum Guide by Ken Schwaber and Jeff Sutherland, the fathers of Scrum, clearly states.

"Scrum is a lightweight framework that helps people, teams, and organizations generate value through adaptive solutions to complex problems."

That is the first sentence of the definition of Scrum from the Scrum Guide 2020. So Scrum is about producing things. So it's essentially a framework for optimizing the delivery process - not a project management methodology. From a

DSDM point of view, what is at the core of Scrum is sort of taking place within Evolutionary Development. Prince2 would simply call it "Delivery" or the "Managing Product Delivery" process. Of course, this cannot substitute an entire project management approach, nor does it want to.

Teams and organizations that use Scrum do so to create products of maximum customer value. While it is certainly possible to extend Scrum and Scrum approaches to enterprise approaches, the fact is that this then represents an extension and is no longer exclusively the Scrum that people learn in Scrum Master training courses from various certifiers.

DSDM goes much further here. As a complete project management method, it offers all elements for project control and since it is an agile project management method, it also offers approaches comparable to Scrum with regard to the realization of products by self-motivated and self-organized teams.

DSDM ® or traditional project management?

If we now compare DSDM with traditional project management, we see that there are comparable approaches in terms of project control, controlling, security, and so on. The big difference lies in the underlying mindset and its implementation in the course of the project. This includes the following points:

ax. The project steering (steering committee, steering group or whatever the role is called in the various methods) is an integral part of the project steering and is thus involved - even if not on a full-time basis - in the progress of the project. This already provides a different awareness and form of cooperation than in project management approaches, where the steering committee essentially only appears in the event of problems or, in the worse case, is conspicuous by its absence even then.

ax. The project manager sees his role not as the leader of the project, but as the facilitator of the process for creating the product. He makes decisions at the project level, but also gives the professionals involved sufficient decision-making authority of their own, on the one hand to increase their identification with the product, and on the other hand to ensure that their skills and knowledge benefit the project not only individually, but also in the synergy of the various roles and skills.

ax. Decisions are made at the appropriate level. Lean would speak of leadership at all levels. In addition to including and fostering a sense of responsibility for their work and the resulting product, this also offers the great advantage of being able to react quickly and purposefully to changes without incurring greater risk.

ax. Through agile procedures and regular feedback loops provided for in the process and learning from experience as fundamental control concepts, it is possible to react faster and more efficiently in the event of deviations, uncertainties or changes occurring, without having to go through any processes that lie outside the project and are therefore difficult to control.

These are just some of the fundamental aspects that speak for the use of an agile project management methodology - and that is DSDM. If, despite this, DSDM is often referred to as hybrid project management, this is often mainly due to a lack of clarity regarding the terms used.

VI

Afterword

This book was announced on the topic of "Hybrid Project Management". Finally, a method for "Agile Project Management" was presented. One may wonder whether this fulfilled the book's value proposition.

In fact, this question is not quite so easy to answer because the term "Hybrid Project Management" is not clearly defined and is used quite differently by different people. From my point of view, it has become apparent in the course of the last few pages that what many people understand by the term "Hybrid Project Management" is actually nothing other than "Agile Project Management" and the claim is essentially based on a misconception of Scrum, Kanban, etc. as project management methods or frameworks.

BIBLIOGRAPHY

- BENTLEY, COLIN. *PRINCE2: A Practical Handbook.* ROUTLEDGE, 2017.
- Chaplin, David. *Prince2®: Se préparer à La Certification Prince2: Concepts De Base, Mots-clés, Principes, thèmes, Processus.* Editions ENI, 2019.
- Craddock, Andrew, et al. *The DSDM Agile Project Framework.* DSDM Consortium, 2012.
- Doerr, John, et al. *OKR - Objectives e'amp; Key Results Wie Sie Ziele, Auf Die Es Wirklich Ankommt Entwickeln, Messen Und Umsetzen.* Verlag Franz Vahlen GmbH, 2018.
- Kaiser, Fabian, and Roman Simschek. *PRINCE2 Die Erfolgsmethode Einfach erklärt. Version 2017.* UVK, 2020.
- Kaiser, Fabian, and Roman Simschek. *PRINCE2 Die Erfolgsmethode Einfach erklärt.* UVK Verlag, 2019.
- Leopold, Martin J. *OKR - Strategy Development and Implementation in an Agile Environment Introduction to the World's Most Successful Framework for Strategy Execution in the 21st Century.* BoD - Books on Demand, 2021.
- Lundberg, Alvar. *Erfolgreich Mit Dem Agilen Spotify Framework Squads, Tribes Und Chapters - Der nächste Schritt Nach Scrum Und Kanban?* BoD - Books on Demand, 2020.
- MULLER, PAUL C. *SCRUM UND KANBAN - DOPPELTER ERFOLG DURCH KOMBINATION: Scrum Und Kanban Erfolgreich Kombinieren -.* BOOKS ON DEMAND, 2021.
- Marfurt, Markus. *Pocket Guide to the Professional Scrum Master Certification (PSM 1).* BoD - Books on Demand, 2020.

BIBLIOGRAPHY

- Müller Mandy, and Mario Kraus. *Scrum in Der Praxis Erfolgreiches Projektmanagement Mit System! Ziele Erreichen, Mitarbeiter Motivieren Und Produktivität Steigern.* Cherry Media GmbH, 2021.
- Müller Paul C. *Agile Leadership in the Scrum Context (Updated for Scrum Guide V. 2020) Servant Leadership for Agile Leaders and Those Who Want to Become One.* BoD - Books on Demand, 2021.
- Müller Paul C. *Scrum Und Kanban - Doppelter Erfolg Durch Kombination (Aktualisiert für Scrum Guide V. 2020) Scrum Und Kanban Erfolgreich Kombinieren - Bessere Prozessbeherrschung Im Sprint - Eine Vorbereitung Auf Die Professional Scrum Kanban (PSK-1)-Zertifizierung.* BoD - Books on Demand, 2021.
- O'Connell, R., and D. J. Tudor. *DSDM: Dynamic Systems Development Method.* National Computing Centre, 1996.
- Richards, Keith, and Maree Richards. *Agile Project Management: Running PRINCE2 Projects with DSDM Atern.* TSO, 2007.
- Richards, Robert M. *DSDM® - Agiles Projektmanagement - Eine (Noch) Unbekannte Alternative Voller Vorteile Eine Einführung in Die AgilePM® Methode, Welche Das Beste Aus Klassischer Projektsteuerung Und Agiler Produktentwicklung Verbindet.* BoD - Books on Demand, 2020.
- Schwaber, Ken, and Jeff Sutherland. *Software in 30 Tagen: Wie Manager Mit Scrum Wettbewerbsvorteile für Ihr Unternehmen Schaffen.* Dpunkt, 2014.
- Stapleton, Jennifer. *DSDM: De Methode in De Praktijk.* Pearson/Addison-Wesley, 2005.
- Sutherland, Jeff, et al. *The Power of Scrum.* CreateSpace, 2011.

www.ingramcontent.com/pod-product-compliance
Lightning Source LLC
Chambersburg PA
CBHW020712180526
45163CB00008B/3046